I0341482

in case of emergency press

We are proud to acknowledge the Traditional Owners of country throughout Australia and to recognise their continuing connection to land, waters, and culture.
We pay our respects to their Elders.

We support recognition, reconciliation, and reparation.

Like a Small City

Carla de Goede

in case of emergency press
https://icoe.com.au
Travancore, Victoria
Australia

Published by in case of emergency press

Copyright © Carla de Goede 2022

All rights reserved. Without limiting the rights under copyright reserved above, no part of this publication may be reproduced, stored in or introduced into a database and retrieval system or transmitted in any form or any means (electronic, mechanical, photocopying, recording or otherwise) without the prior written permission of both the owner of copyright and the above publishers.

ISBN: 978-0-6453751-9-0

Acknowledgements

Like a Small City, shortlisted for the Dorothy Hewett Award 2022
The Cleaning Woman, Third Place, June Shenfield Poetry Award 2020
Hospital, Maggots and His Face, Third Place, Maureen Freer Poetry Award 2020
Sonnet of my Returned Self, published The Victorian Writer Dec 2020
In the arm chair, Highly Commended, The Ethel Webb Bundell Poetry Award 2020
Cats, shortlisted Ada Awards 2020
On Becoming a Poet, First Place, Positive Words Xmas Competition 2020
The Felt Hat, published Woorilla Awards 2021
How to Write a Poem in a time of Argument, published Woorilla Awards 2021
Letter of Reckoning, published Woorilla Awards 2021
Womb, published Woorilla Awards 2021

Dedication

For all those who believed in me.

And for you, dear reader.

Table of Contents

At Two 1
On Doubt 3
Escape 5
The Felt Hat 6
When I go Insane 7
The Derelict Well in the City 8
The Cleaning Woman 9
Winter Afternoon 12
Pieces of Spring 14
She imagines herself a Kite 16
Hands, Crabs and Hindsight 17
Suburbia after the Party 18
Remembrance 19
Conundrum 20
Sunday 22
Yes and How? 25
Over 26
Love poem of Goodbye 28
Curtains 30
Ode to an Abandoned House 32
Leaf City 34
Changing Seasons 36
New Father 37
The Evening Star and the Crab Apple Trees 39
Forest 41
Sticking an Owl in 42
Woman standing on a balcony 43
Poetry 44
The Lake 45
Things in the grass that roll over 47
What happened last night 48
Excuse for not attending class 50
Letter of Reckoning 51
Out of the Clouds 52
Adoption 55
Fire 57

Hospital, Maggots and His Face	58
Chained Inside	59
Three Shades of Lemonade	62
Sonnet of my Returned Self	64
Untitled Mess	65
What Writing feels like	67
The Mountain	69
The crumpled people huddle	71
In the arm chair	72
Watching…	75
The Last Breath	76
Wake	77
Morning Under a Bridge	78
Aubade	80
Cats	82
Arms	83
Red	84
Journey out the back door…	86
Arthritis, Boats and Red Jam	88
What poetry does	90
Bite	91
Dear Separation,	93
The Meaning	95
Dollies, War and Pillars	96
At Four, Learning Poetry	99
How to Write a Poem in a Time of Argument	101
The girl-moth	103
The New Beginning	104
Four Vignettes	106
On Becoming a Poet	113
The Horse that Knows More	115
The Last Day	117
Womb	119
On Encouragement	120
About the Author	121

Like a Small City

Carla de Goede

At Two

When she
was sent a-
way—

out went her con-
fid-
ence,

out went her voice.

How she travelled
from Melbourne to Canberra
on the taste of alcohol

to a green pot
up against a cold back door…

Though she did not
need to go
she sat through—

an old woman
licking her lips,

guests arriving.
Having a cup of tea,

eating lunch
and staring at her…

Eyes, eyes, eyes

Till finally
the new adult said

'enough'

and she was
allowed to come
away from the draft

into a childhood of

stutt-
er-
ing

and fear
of
the shower.

On Doubt

You come in like an old woman—
clothes crumpled and out of place.
Meander like a Parkinson's patient
stop/start across my page.
Tell me that my voice is stuffed
and will never have the flow
of a newly laid pipe.

Meanwhile, the garden is full of bees
buzzing their anthem.

I sit like a cat and wait patiently
for you to crash your walker
into one of the holes of my page.
Cos I'm gonna write no matter what.
Even if I have to perambulate
through seven poems
of disaster and strange pauses.

You snicker and say 'Your brain is snuffed.'
I look at you with my cat eyes—
unblinking but full of terror,
'what if you're right and this is
the last line
I ever
write?'…

'No! You don't fool me.'

I lick my paws
and begin again—
(stepping carefully
on your wheels)

and just like that
Doubt
hobb-
les
a-
way.

Escape

1)
She fell out of his
'can't do that body stoppered hallway',
out of his
'phone monitored have to be silent',
out of his
car
rolling for life,
away from his gun.
How she fell—

the gutter was so suddenly there
banging hard on her arm
stretching out like a cliff.

His laughter cracked.

She saw herself
upside down
in the mirror,
felt
warm blood
on her cheek

then he was gone.

2)
On the side of the road
she is a fan—
one moment crying,
one moment shaking.

A fan—
old, discarded junk.

3)
She doesn't know where she is…

The Felt Hat

Disguised as a hat I am going to rip your eyebrows off
and put a deep shadow across your forehead.

You won't see me coming—I'll look all innocent in the wind.
And besides, your head will be bowed down as it always is
when you shuffle along.

Maybe you will be thinking about your boat, how it needs a new
motor or the photos on your desk or even the latest dog race.

Maybe you won't be thinking anything at all. Just watching
the leaves scrunch beneath your feet like little deaths.

But I am coming with my dark, brooding thoughts and my best
felt attire.
I am coming when the wind howls its ghostly cries.
I am coming and there's no escape.

I shall hat you down man
and brim your eyes with regret.

When I go Insane

I will wear a space suit
with an umbrella
and make hyper-jumps
to the shopping centre
where I will buy
donuts
with exactly
89
sprinkles
and half a chicken-goose.

I will borrow a mobile
just to talk to a stranger.
Then I will get some paint
and scrawl
'I'm alive'
on the pavement.

Then I'll paint
half my face
(the top half)
and sing
a song
about
orange fish.

Then I'll catch a train to
somewhere else
and watch the cops
fly.

The Derelict Well in the City

I put my fake ego in my holster
and swagger into the poetry room
trailing hills, sheep and grass
like the country boy I am.

I fidget with my fake ego
point it ruefully at the girl
I have followed here
only to meet the eye

of a man
trailing buildings, concrete and bitumen.
Then there's his muscle —
three sides of sideways.

Then, just as I'm about to beat
a hasty retreat
the sun slides in
trailing pens, paper and textas.

Gosh, she smells of
frangipanes and vanilla.
And that's how
I came to be writing this poem

scraping ink together
like I know what I'm doing.

Like a Small City

The Cleaning Woman

It was a cloudless morning—
wind like an elephant's
trumpet
scraping the windows, making them sing.

She, carrying a vacuum cleaner
boarded the train
like a strange octopus
with too many legs

of fabric and cloth.
One was a bucket.
Another a brush.

She stood where she always stood—
(too much stuff poking this way
and that to sit down).

The windows tat, tat, tat-ing.
The train whale singing
its protests.

Over to her right—
passenger sleeping.

Over to her left—
man hallucinating sharks and
bombs and poisoned carrots.

'You carrot, I'll get ya.'

She turns away.

'I've got a bomb
and I'll shark it to ya'.

The passengers—dreary morning
sleep sacks
keep their eyes
on phones
or out the windows

where skyscrapers
flash by like
little flotillas
of life.

They run like
concrete emus

in a desert landscape

and she's back to a holiday
she took last Summer

with Fred and Marge
and the yellowness of the sun
filling the whole sky like
a crazy canary
stalking them for lunch.

'I'll get ya' the man says again.

The doors open—Alley Barber of
colours pour in,
Alley Barber of colours
pour out.

The woman—octopussing up
too much space
goes out,
smiling her apologies

to the mad,
thrumming crowd.

Then

bang

the blackness comes down
like a photographic cloth

and she, pavement prone
is a puddle of vacuum-cleaner,
buckets
and
rags…

Winter Afternoon

The clouds are as busy as
passengers at a
train station…

I sit beneath them
so old now that
all I want to do

is curl up with a book
near a snuggle warm fire
and let my mind go…

Only problem is
I can't seem to focus.
The words roll over me

like hallucinations

and I read the same sentence
three or four times
without any…

Sometimes, my eyes drift
to the window
where they might see

dog
or sky
or trees…

I am drifting again
to a fight we had
last night
and who said what
to whom

and I can't remember…

Only the pain.

The clouds
drop
suitcases of change
onto our lives

as you enter
the asylum
involuntarily.

Pieces of Spring

The tulips bend in the wind —
whispering to the soil
about slugs and sawdust.

A magpie struts down
the driveway — little tank
on patrol.

A dog jumps in the air
turning like a frisbee
after a ball.

The sky — a blue bowl
over everything
seems to smile

and the sun
hovers
like a helicopter

then rolls up his sleeves
like a gardener
overturning a wheelbarrow.

A couple kiss for the first time —
tongues tasting like M and M's
and cola.

From next door
the smell of a BBQ
and the splash of a pool.

The blossom tree shakes
a magic carpet down
on everything.

The bees zing
their mystery
around the flowers

and everything holds
its breath
while a new egg

of possibility
is placed in
every nest.

Then the gardener
shadows the wheelbarrow
and disappears behind

the hills…

She imagines herself a Kite

She sits in her wheelchair
hiding in the shadow while
everyone plays.

In her head there's a-
mazing things:
a
group of kids
include her, she's the
next hero,
everyone is friendly and
she's special. But really she's

hiding from
everyone, their
razor,
sharp,
electric
language
forbidding her to join in.

All of them together,

killing her
inspiration
to
ever fly.

Hands, Crabs and Hindsight

Dear Hands,

        you sit there, silently not moving—attached to his sides like dead fish. He, psychopath, keeps you still as fishing poles so as not to give himself away. But I know better. In my dreams I have seen you—shadow-creeping across the wall—two crabs moving against the current of moonlight. I have seen you creep round the bookshelf and strangle it so that books fall eerily out of it.
And once I saw you paint the wall red with your butcher's uniform as you carelessly threw it aside.
But I have also seen you carefully take a lettuce out of the ground—holding it like a precious child. And fix the car—lovingly caressing it.
However, now that you are dead, the ants of our lives have come out to haunt me—biting me with the truth. They creep—black, six-legged things sucking the last of the rose-coloured sugar out of our relationship and I am left with the question: to donate or not to donate your hands to your brother?
Meanwhile, your hands wonder through my memories like debris floating to the surface in the river of hindsight. How you put them round my neck and squeezed over and over again. Conscious, not conscious—a traffic light—one globe away from gone.
Now you sit there, even more silently than before and I must choose to donate or not to donate as you reach like a pair of vultures round the neck of my memories, pecking all hope apart and leaving me crab-shell empty.

Suburbia after the Party

Windows—
women clad
in dressing gowns
sticking their noses out...

Garbage bins,
knocked over again.

Infants
being marched
to the kindergarten
at the end of the road.

One lone Tom
dali-timed out of place
still howls for a mate.

Cars pass
like nothing is out of place

and the graffiti says
'get fucked'
in the middle of the street.

Bottles of aftermath
roll into piles.

The postman wheels his bike
scared of the glass.

He—
window
furtively looking in

on dishevelled carnage.

It was beautiful yesterday.

Remembrance

What if you knew you'd be
the last person to touch someone?

Would your hand linger on their cheek
like a flower pushing through
the dust…

as if you could write hidden words
with your hands,

weave them out of skin
so that
your hand print would remain

forever, a bird settling down
to roost…

and out of the fabric of its nest,
out of the fabric of dust

the words 'I love you'.
Those words

that you never say anymore
would burn bright

like baubles and Christmas lights…

But instead
you did not know

and can only line the coffin
with forget-me-knots

and a whispered apology…

Conundrum

The gumtrees rise
like white ghosts
touching the sun
that flies like an eagle.

Like white ghosts
they flutter songs
that fly like an eagle
across the sky.

They flutter songs
like 'shush'
across the sky
as loud as any cityscape.

Like 'shush'
and one koala
as loud as any cityscape
pisses down an awareness.

And one koala
eats a gum leaf
pisses down an awareness
like a pocket of sense.

Eats a gum leaf
that scientists think is toxic.
Like a pocket of sense
it still exists.

That scientists think is toxic
but what do they know?
It still exists
like a kite stuck in a tree.

But what do they know?
In their lab coats,
like a kite stuck in a tree
how wrong they are.

In their lab coats
making no progress.
How wrong they are
these men who can bend light.

Making no progress,
touching the sun
these men who can bend light.
The gum trees rise.

Sunday

Moonlight,
me
and the hard
slats of a bench.

The trees lean in,
priests
over a casket.

Flutteringly I sleep.

I'm in a room
with a tear

fall-
ing
down
the
wall,
thin
as a spider's web.

There's a table
and a long
glass vase
with a single
black rose.

I sit beneath
the table.

A spider scuttles
underneath
the door.

Like a Small City

From outside
the waves
crash rock.

And a single car
grizzles along.

Another tear
drops.

I freeze into
an ice-block
and the moonlight
forms bright bars
across my square frame.

Then my mother enters
the room,
sticks a label
'To Antarctica'
over my left eye

and disappears into
the mist.

Then a single black
petal falls
over my right eye.

I awake
in a single sheet
of moonlight,

breath—
cold

and white
like a ghost
es-
cap-
ing
in-
to
the
night.

And overhead
the hover
of priests
snarl.

Yes and How?

Two heads on a pillow
looking up at the sky…

He thought 'Yes I'm a man now.'
She thought 'How did that happen?'
and the breeze licked the leaves.

Earlier he had been ordinary—
following rules and studying hard.

She had been falling into a depression
thinking of the father who had left her.

He drifted off into a superhero slumber
where all the girls were chasing him.

She tried not to cry, thinking
she didn't even love him

and the night folded in on them
like a charcoal drawing.
Nothing was real anymore.

She put her clothes back on
and staggered away.

One head on a pillow
and the rooster crowed
'light'.

Then a single
twig snapped…

Over

The door mat
looked at her man—
eyes
strawed open.
How she wanted him
big and strong.

She'd type up his poems
one by one,
send out all his emails

and smiled on.

Then she came up
with ideas
to enhance his career.

More work for her—
no problem,

he would grow big and strong.

But the door mat
weaved her own words—
thought her man
was big and strong,
would
support her too.
But the man
was not really a big man
and wiped his feet
all over her.

Like a Small City

The door mat turned her face
to the ground
covered her
'welcome home'
and cried her stupid tears.

In the shade
of her proneness
a little power grew.

She shook herself
and rearranged her letters into
'moor dat'

and the little man
could no longer
send out his work
because his girl hands
were gone.

She had left him for poetry—
the lines, the words
the embraces
she never really had.

Go
'moor dat'.
'Welcome Home'.

Love poem of Goodbye

For the lover in my past

*If I could rewrite your life
I would put a happy face on your wall
and undo the nails in your coffin…*

You would remember how
I began with yellow
and added a smile to your sun.

How it would watch over you
and your father would not
have nailed you in your cot.

But then maybe
I would not have met
your love
that still reaches out to grow…

If I had been your Mary
and you my treasured junior
I would have had the love

to grow your sleeping apart
with a new picture each day:
sun, fire engine, sailing boat.

Then I would watch you bob
out across the years
into a happy, long term relationship.

But in a time when
I was escaping
my 18th birthday

planned to ball
in a hall of lonely men

that somehow turned into
a 1:00pm time slot
leave before 6:00 thing…

And escaping my childhood time
of male and female
wandering hands…

And escaping almost two
when I called my mother
a cow—

my first metaphor
for being sent away
and replaced by a new baby.

Throughout all those years
we both lost confidence
and the voice to unravel
our differences.

And then with a thunderclap
your self-esteem plummeted
and my book got held back…

and we, only people
survivors of the mad
crashed upon the rocks.

But now I rewrite your life,
type in self esteem
like I'm growing a new plant

and wish your soil
full of love.

Curtains

Somewhere in a room
far, far away
there's a poet like me.

He s-t-r-e-t-c-h-e-s out
like a seven
in front of his desk

stuck in the middle
of a—
Outside,

fog runs like
stein bock
from the sun.

He shivers.
She is the sky,
blue
in her l-i-n-g-e-r-i-e

Why did he let her go?

He looks at a note
from a teacher:

'A planet is like a cherry.
Space them out properly
or the vine
becomes drunk
and far too sickly sweet.'

But how do you capture a woman?

Like a Small City

Throw her on the page
like confetti
so she can't get back
and lodge
again
in his head.

He looks at the cactus
she left behind
and he is dry,
so dry for a
kiss.

He was such a silly stag
running from the only sun
who left him alone
to write.

Women like that
are cherries
in the cycle
of one night stars.

Somewhere in a room
far, far away
a man pulls the curtains
shut.

There are no words
for the poem
of a woman.

Ode to an Abandoned House

You whistle through my dreams like
a small city—

door clattering as if alive.
You swim before me

and heave open that old argument
that went round like a yo-yo

and broke us apart
(him turning to alcohol

me stuck with the kids).
Now you are all dark windows

and skulking cats.
Needles

and caulky faces
heaving in the corners.

But once you were
a girl on a swing,

a boy on a
slide—

before the bank crumpled you
into dereliction

with an overseas buyer
unable to care for you.

But still I dream
your dark windows

will be light
when a new family

moves in.
The trees nonchalantly

make their stand
and thicken up around you…

Leaf City

My pile of leaves looks like a draft city—
red people on the inside,
yellow and brown on the outside.

No white people to make it all collapse.

The trees flicker their leaves and
make the draft city glow
with possibilities...

Suddenly,
I'm standing on the cobblestones
and sprawl of my imagined city

where brown is beautiful
and no Tom or Peter
steals my lunch...

I sit at the front of
the bus—
princess

with no draw-bridge of feet
to clamber over.

The trees yawn above me
and I wonder if
this had been my life

would I be
an easy-going leaf
on the wind of life?

Like a Small City

Or would I still be
morse-coded with tension
in every pocket of my being

like a voodooed
jack-in-the-box?

A magpie pecks at my
draft city

and pulls me back
to the pain of black and white.

Then it warbles hope back
for a better tomorrow

and I head into my
counsellor's office
to remove some pins
from my life…

and think how
the lack of pigment in skin
might make white people
an afterthought
to live in cities
where light is less abundant

while we were here first.

Changing Seasons

In the heart of a rose
a tear-drop—
that rainbow colour
of possibility.

My life—
a cloudy,
glass jar
opens
and the scent
of trees

hugs me.
I am in new-birth
and push forward
an octopus tentacle
(previously arthritic)
unfurling
for the first time,

escaping a coffin-box
with new medication.

The rose flutters
in the wind.
My nose follows
the scent

like a loose leaf
overturning
again

and the trees whisper
'yes'
like a society of old women

ready to be friends…

Like a Small City

New Father

You dream in circles
like a boxed in camper.
Fire eats your belly
as smoke dribbles before you.

Like a boxed in camper
you wake, a nightmare
as smoke dribbles before you,
the light illuminates your face.

You wake, a nightmare
The curtains flap the window
as light illuminates your face.
She stirs next to you.

The curtains flap the window.
The moon, a bulldozer.
She stirs next to you
and you want to run away.

The moon a bulldozer
cutting back in history
and you want to run away.
Back to no responsibilities,

cutting back in history
when you freely ate apples.
Back to no responsibilities
and the hay you rolled in

when you freely ate apples
and had any girl.
And the hay you rolled in
everything was all yours.

And had any girl
before your father died.
Everything was all yours.
Beginnings impossible to stop

before your father died.
School seemed unimportant.
Beginnings impossible to stop
were doled out like smarties.

School seemed unimportant.
Fire eats your belly.
The room weighs down on you.
You dream in circles.

The Evening Star and the Crab Apple Trees

When they stole her children
the white walls leaned in—
zeitgeists of the time
while a shiver ran out the door.

There she lay—
under anaesthetic
half dreaming
of a beach with waves coming in,

the smell of crab apple trees
in the distance
and the evening star
pressing its light down

from the ceiling.
In her mind she was
naming the children
Jenny and Louise.

Had a photo album
now empty
five weeks later
and still the tears

spluttered like an old candle…
She imagined
every knock
at the door

was him coming back.
How he'd look hollowed out
as if a whole highway
had roaded itself

through him—
He'd get down on one knee
and she'd say yes
just so she could have

Louise and Jenny back.

She had no placenta
to plant something with
but still she planted
two crab apple trees.

Then on her fiftieth birthday
a letter came
that sent her back to the beach
with its waves of nausea…

She stood with the evening star
blinking out a positive future
holding a crab apple tree
for each of them.

Though their names were different
they stood—strong women
slightly aloof
before she hugged them

for the first time.
The scent of their crab apple perfume

surprisingly linking them in
to the family tree.

Forest

If you go into the woods today you will find:
mushrooms
gorging on a fallen tree
dangerous as tarantulas,

ants working together like
innocuous daisy chains,

trees leaning in
like soldiers
of dark thoughts…

and the path will wind—
a snake
about your ankles.

The water from the waterfall
will remind you
of a bride falling backwards…

into life
as you come up and take
your first breath
after lockdown.

But beware
the shadow
who stalks you—

bare arms
like an open prison

and the trees lean in
as shots
fire…

Sticking an Owl in

Writing poetry used to be easy.
I'd pick up some ripple in the universe—
a wave coming in and surf it all the
way to the shore without changing my
makeup…

But then again, I never worried about
if the owl was in its proper place
or apples were on the apple tree
or if I put the car in the right
garage. I'd simple write and
whallah—a garden full of sunlight

or a building falling over,
stray hat on the pavement.
And I wouldn't worry about a thing.
But now I am trying to edit it all
down to a single bit of essence
that you can put in your mouth
and suck like a lozenge—solid at first
then hot, hot, hot…

And connecting the metaphor
like an owl out of place
is just so hard that I feel like
I've gone back to working with
a feather and a tied-up brain
that will not break through
its cerebellum of disappointment.

Woman standing on a balcony

She holds her arms out to the sun
    so that a huge bird shadow
    appears on the pavement below

    where a bin—full to the brim
    stenches the street like
    a drunk man urinates

    marking his territory like
    Jesus anoints the children
    with a heart and a kiss.

    From somewhere a rat
    slithers in the undercurrent—
    eyes shiny as knives

She leans like a donkey
the woman on the balcony
almost, almost leaning off…

    into her history
    where a man—knife out
    lunged

and her stomach…
No children

Poetry

is a one sock guy
getting off at Flinders.

His hair, sticky and elongated
carries cobwebs like

the corner of a broom cupboard
crossed with the Dandenong Ranges.

He has come to play the violin
in Bourke St Mall.

Poetry
is a tiny, grasshopper woman
hauling a piano

like some shell of despair
over the tram tracks.

She, mad dung beetle
dragging a big brown thing

while pedestrians go by like
speeding skinks.

Poetry
is when the two meet
and the man
throws his violin
at the piano.
Oh the falsetto scream!

The Lake

Suddenly, happiness took me
like a man with strong arms.

The wind ripples the lake
as if a child
stirred it
with a stick…

The pelicans snap—
a parading marching band.

All around couples
with masks on
hold hands

as the sun dips into the water
like a flamingo.

Fire worms dance on the lake
and sea gulls—
those garbage bags of the sky
tear the remains of fish
to shreds.

I want to catch the scene
with my paint brush
in azure blue and
crimson red

but had left the paints behind
along with the malaise
of lockdown…

but still

suddenly, happiness took me
like a man with strong arms

and together
we went dancing
round
the lake.

Things in the grass that roll over

I am seven years old
making pictures
out of clouds:

a bike,
seven laughing girls
and a bucket with a hole in it.

In my mouth
I chew a sour sob
just to be cool.

The sun,
peaking shyly out
is my only friend.

From inside I can hear
'I want a divorce'
and
'What about the kids?'

and
my brother and his friends
fly past on their bikes.

The dog
chases its tail
missing
every time

like nothing is happening…

My mind is that bucket
and I am weeping through
strange holes
and can not stop…

What happened last night

I come with ten weeping lines
tucked under my arm
—a folder of nonsense
to share with a class
I hardly know.

How the lines sit
like sailors,
heavy against my chest.

The algebra circles
round like strange pictures
and makes no sense.

Recess is like
a heavy dip in tar
until the football
smashes the glass

and I decide
to leg it
so I would not
have to share:

father like a helicopter saw
flung my arms
across the room—
severed our relationship
with a whisky
and a kite

I tremble still—
my head like a
boxed up chandelier
lights half out.

Like a Small City

The sailors
row my confidence away
with things I dare not share

in case whisky
is there again

and I will fly—
stupid, crumpled body
who forgot to hide.

Excuse for not attending class

After the alarm did not go off
my limbs were rigid —
felt like they had turned
paper thin…

When I carefully looked in the
dresser mirror (with a heavy ache
in my head)
I found them to be brown…

Then I realised I'd turned
into a tree! Not a pine tree
or a gum tree but a paperbark tree
and the ants were eating my bark.

I watched them carefully
slice my bark with their mandibles
and pass it to the next ant
(It hurt like hell, over and over again.)

I wondered why I still had eyes
and then I figured my transformation
was incomplete and I dreaded going
back to sleep…

I nodded this way and that
from the breeze that came in
through the open window
but no matter how hard I tried

I could not get up.

Then my bladder exploded
(which I apparently still had too)

and I just was in no state to attend
class.

Letter of Reckoning

Dear Under-the-Bridges,
                       I have seen you playing—old, rusty bikes going like ninjas through the wind. I have seen you fire lighting the night with old drums, stringing up like yo-yos to each other to tell stories—voices droning on into the night like broken diesel engines and I imagine what it would be like to give one of you a home.

How you would sit there like a hippo—not moving, wary of your new pond. Scarf like a new flag tying you to great expectations. How you would look at me like I was an ant ready to be squashed.

And slowly, slowly, I imagine you would say something about your life—how you had killed a homeless man or raped a child. How you carried a knife as a mascot and had an evil eye for everyone cos everyone's just out to get everyone else.

How you'd say that I just wanted you for sex or the money the government will pay and you'd hard nose look at me like I was the devil.

How to love a creature like that? Feed him pasta and fish and chips. Let him drink a little cola and tell him he is special. Ask him what his dreams are.

But he will laugh at you and return to his friends under the bridge for more drugs and subhuman ways.

Oh, but in my imagination how you will roll over into a new life. But my dreams shatter like dying stars as I see you needle up yet again.

Out of the Clouds

Imagination grows by
sloshing through puddles,

by taking umbrellas
for a spin round
the garden,

by sitting on a bench
and watching:

a man whispering
in a woman's
ear,

a train trundling past—
passengers like
headless
zombies,

a donkey
braying for
an apple…

and I'm back
in Bethlehem
trading donkeys

chickens and goats
like a BC farmer.
Eyes on

coloured
silks

I'll never own
as the sands

massage my feet…
I'm back

on a beach
in modern times

watching
sailboats—

gutses out like
Santa Clauses…

The pine tree
is decorated
in the city square

and suddenly
I'm four years old
and my mother
is lost…

I see flashy pink
high heel
shoes,

sneakers
and

I don't know
which way to go.

The miniature train
goes choo-choo
past the window

and the lights
of the town
are on.

Like a Small City

Everybody is holding
somebody else's
hand.

I look
at the sky —

the sun
slinks back
into the horizon —

yellow rag
scrubbing
the pinkness
out.

Now, shadows
curl
like
ghosts

and I'm sloshing
in a puddle,

catch
the train
back
to the beginning
and…

Adoption

'How old are you?' the boy said
messily colouring a tree.

'I'm as old as the planets
and as young as a newborn babe',

the woman said, drawing a cubby house
to go in the boy's tree.

'No you're not,'
said the boy, pushing his truck

over the paper.
'Yes. I'm made of stardust.'

The boy thought for a moment
and said

'I'm made of water
and thousands of pikelets.

That's my favourite food.
With jam.'

But in reality, the boy had
never had any pikelets,

hadn't eaten much
apart from chips

and a little bread.
His stomach rumbled

like a concrete mixer
into his mother

unable to be woken,
stretched out on the couch.

He pulled the curtains down
on the memory

and listlessly wheeled his truck
trying to tear the paper.

'Would you like to live with me?'
the woman asked

but the boy left the question hanging like a broken coat hanger.

'We could build this
in a tree' the woman said.

'Only if I can have a telescope
and we can paint stars over it.'

The woman smiled
'But you have to help me build it.'

Fire

Today I want to hit something…
I am all tears in a coffee pot,

mad vegetable cut into soup,
soggy bread without crust.

He is out there again
like the fence has a new post…

I'm late
but he sits on my day

like a wet Kleenex
or a car without a battery.

He connects the grassy paddock of yesteryear
with a crumbling cliff of today

and no matter what I do
I cannot shake that bastard

from my front lawn.
I call the police yet again.

I'll be late for work and
at the rate I'm going

I'll lose my job by the end of the week.
How I want to hit something

as he stands there, nonchalantly
all owl (in his own head at least).

Hospital, Maggots and His Face

Her dreams are like:
tumbleweeds through a desert,
oranges on a lemon tree,
a guinea pig in a maggots' nest,
a big truck going the wrong way,
a rat being eaten by a snake,
bears in the wrong country,
baked beans fried in ten-day old oil,
a queue of vegetarians
at the butcher's,
and a spaceman out of his rocket

and she always wanted out—
Tossed and turned like a
pogo stick on the floor-thin mattress...

but the Son of the Third Reich
kept on
ECTing her

till one day
it all just stopped

except for His Face
that haunted
her space
like a Giant
Billboard.

Chained Inside

*Summer—
that lizard neck of
dry*

*has me pinned
inside
like an insect*

*dropped
on a
specimen page.*

My shadow
circles under
my bed

like a restless panther
chained to
a no-win situation.

Then I cry
in my locked-in
syndrome

as the nurses
hurry by
not knowing

I am here,
panther-
insect

try-ing to t-alk.

The curtains billow
like a cheer squad
of possibilities.

But how do you move
when you've forgotten
what that even feels like?

'I'm right here'
I scream
on my internal

throat walls,
slap at a fly
without moving my hand.

'I'm right here'
I whisper
on my internal

throat walls.
But no one comes
as the sun

presses its head in
to find out
what's going on.

And I collapse again
into myself
like a pudding

that's undercooked
and ask the sun
to take me soon

as my shadow
makes another slow lap
around my bed…

Then the sun
turns to moon
turns to sun.

Three Shades of Lemonade

*The film of her life
is stuck to the glass jar*

visible and unrecognisable.

She had lemons all
cut, ready to make
lemonade

but in the glass jar
a man—
fat-faced and bearded
stares at her.

How long must she wait
for the ghost
to leave?

Again she finds herself
flat on her back
in hospital,

face like mangled metal
only able to drink liquids.

Her mother came and brought
lemonade

while her daughter brought
chrysanthemums and
a worried smile.

She kept asking herself
'why?' like a stupid
door,

opening and closing
on a question

that had no answer.

And here he was again
in the glass jar

that should have been
a positive memory,

screaming his obscenities
and pounding her face.

He was always punching her
face
though it happened
only once.

The curtains dance
innocently in the breeze

and she wanted to tear
their insides apart

so maybe then
she'd be able to
go out again…

… or finish making
lemonade.

Sonnet of my Returned Self

Now my sentences are like fences.
They are strong enough to pen sheep

or build tall buildings from scratch.

I can put a woman on a ball
on the top floor with pink leotards.

Or I can put an octopus at the bottom of a rock pool.

Watch as I tumble rocks
without taking a breath.

Or collide two cars
without any injuries.

Because each word
is no longer a barb
in my fences,

my synapses are electric…

Untitled Mess

After the last psychopath walked through me
i have been living like an abandoned house—
shattered walls,
the dirty squalor,
soul half thrown through the window.

And he of course
goes on living—
New friends,
new choir,
new writing group.

And i am left
wheelchair woman,
wheelchair poverty.
Moving, moving,
always moving.
One step away from homelessness…

And I should be glad I escaped with my life.
After all, if I had had a daughter…
He is the kind of man who would throw her off a bridge,
run her over, or simply make her disappear.

I know this. I know it.
He raped me once in the middle of the desert
'Stop' i said
'Stop'.
'It's alright, it's alright, it's alright' he said.
'Stop' i screamed. Tears and pain in my eyes
But i
pinned down could not move
and he rode on and on through the night
and i was left

sand-scratched
inside
and sore
for two weeks.

And I should be glad I escaped with my life.
But I am a poet
who no longer believes in love.
Which of course is the most ridiculous
oxymoron of all.

Wheelchair woman,
wheelchair woman
your life is still spinning.
You need to get up
and make yourself
live again.

What Writing feels like

Imagine a swamp —
puddles of quicksand
all around

just waiting for your feet
to slip…

The sky is an overhanging
barrel of laughs

and you are
stuck,
stuck,
stuck.

That's how it feels
when your best poems
are rejected

and your shadow
lets go
to cling to
someone else.

Now,
alone
turning to swamp

your toes curl round
a new blade of grass
and a poem
like mist
comes in
over

Like a Small City

the horizon

and everything
starts again...

The Mountain

I am in the tired part of my brain
where sentences do not connect up
and my eyes close like blinds on
a summer's day.

The dog—personality like a dozen
fried eggs, is silent today
so I drift off into…

a mountain—snow capped
with a backpack stuck
in the middle of it.

I am travelling through the
Andes—able bodied at last
going on a holiday I have always
dreamed about.

Talking to my guide like a
babbling brook. Happiness—
a wind with warm arms
dances within me.

I make a snowball
like I am yesterday's age
and sing like there is no
short-
age
of
ox-
y-
gen.

Like a Small City

The dog barks up my dream
and I'm left staring
at my mother's
sheet
over
her junk
heap.

Like a Small City

The crumpled people huddle

in doorways
like brooms.

How their stomachs rumble,
big—as the train going past.

The trees in the rich gardens
lean in—

police officers on patrol.
'No parking, no stopping here,'

they whisper in the wind,
flapping their green talons

about to throw flower
missiles to dispense a crowd.

The crumpled people shed
a single tear

(or is it the wind
eating their eyes)

and move on—

a dust cloud of
slaves

or else
they
lean further into
the doorways

where they die like
saggy, hessian sacks

of never wases.

In the arm chair

He sits in a field of memories.
They grow like tulips—
here for a moment, then gone.

The gills of the house
rattle
with children's laughter

and he struggles
to catch
a
breath.

Once he ran a marathon.
Now his legs are
use-
less.

He is in dry dock,
off
from work
by doctor's orders…

Restless
as a bear
looking for a den.

He is angry mostly
and throws cups
like a yahoo.

They crack
as his mind cracks…

He wishes he could take it back.
All of it.

But he cannot control the impulses anymore
and they rise like stupid waves
until he is a tsunami—

a cup throwing monster
screaming for life.

Five years ago
his work introduced
the stupid pizza checker

and his head has been
absorbing radiation ever since.

He should have gone on strike,
found another job…

but lazy and needing the money
he had stayed.

Now he is restless
as a bear
looking for a place
to die.

He throws the book
he can no longer read
across the room.

It shatters a vase
and his memories
spill like tulips:

getting his science degree,
meeting Mindy,
working the late shifts—
headaches every night.

All of them are
already fading
as his brain
slowly dies.

He's left with two questions:
how to get compensation
and how to tell the children?

The tears come like
fat frogs
ribbetting at his heart.

He knocks the jug
across the room
and the walls cry too.

He cannot die at home.
He is too much out of control.

Bloody brain tumour

and the gills of the house
rattle
with children's laughter…

Watching...

The dishevelled bird
hops over the rocks—

undergarments showing
like the insides of a car.

How long will it hop?

The moon shines down
on blood left behind

and I,
on a beach

of the mind
watch waves

of change
hurtling themselves

at rocks.
I kamikaze

smash with the waves
over my decision

of euthanasia
and what

I will leave
behind...

The Last Breath

Purple comes like mist over the sea.

The pelicans hold their breath
and the sea gulls stop fighting
for just
a
moment.

The salty air changes direction
and the sea rushes away
from shore—

a departing
gaggle of people
stuck
in traffic

—and thinks again of the shore,

rushes back
filling the sand puddles
with a
cacophony of sound.

This is evening.
The time when
all things are possible.

But nothing can be done
stuck on the shore,
painted
into the scene.

Wake

She held the arm with the bruise
like a walkie talkie up to her lips.

The room magnified around her—
the dressing table with its ransacked drawers,

the toilet brush, she'd been welted with
and the baby still asleep in its crib.

Her lip peeled back and bleeding, trembled
So it had come to this…

It was time to leave.
The room spun and she was not sure

if she was really awake
but she felt alive if only by a whisker.

'Jesus give me strength,' she whispered
and the light shone through the curtain

and into the dresser
like an angel unspooling its wings

and she followed the thread
like a hungry caterpillar

devouring every ounce of light
before she fell back on the bed

unconscious…

Morning Under a Bridge

The 'thankyou woman'
wakes up in the dust of a bridge —
traffic rattling past...

Today she will go
busking again.

The sun makes mirages
on the edge of the shadows,

flipping her mind back
to a house where she used to live.

A snail stares at her.
She lifts her foot —
crushes

the husband who went
with other women
and wanted to prostitute
her to friends,

'out damn snail,' she says
'out brief candle'

and the traffic roars
while she washes her face.

'It's today,' the woman says.

Her shirt, dusty,
jeans full of holes...

but still it's today
and she hasn't been
mugged in a while.

The sun picks at her guitar
and the frets grin like
a mouth full of gold teeth…

The woman utters her
'thankyou prayer'
that everyone on the street knows,

curls up
and goes back
to sleep.

Aubade

The alarm clock—
red, devil flashes across my soul.

You, beached whale
snore gently across your pillow…
Morse Code
for me alone.

The curtains billow softly—
rose
emanates from your skin.

I watch the sun reach out its hand
across the dresser
and into the mirror

where it, too bright
mocks my sleepy trance.

If I could, I would tell you
of the chooks in the yard,
the lambs about to spring forth,
planets being built…

but I am silent
in the afterglow of you
and want you all over again…

However, I must
stoke the fire,
make guacamole
and remove the wallpaper.

Ah Big Fish
my fingers are back to last night
trawling your skin
and wanting to come in—

close to your heart
so I can read it
with a thermometer…

But I must go
into the stupid day

and hope you will come back
and glow my evenings
with new light.

Cats

Words are guests
in my mouth.

They come and go
like soldiers on the field.

When they are all gone,
I am barren

and point to things—
mad canary

over pruning its legs
and gasping for breath.

Some days
half the soldiers stay

and I have
every second word or so.

But the best days
are when the adjectives

purr in like cats
then I'm happy

writing a poem
or two…

Arms

'Considering the alternative, it's not too bad at all.'
Maurice Chevalier

The room could be
full of
pins,
lactic acid
and beans.

It could be
full of Dalmatians,
tiger teeth
and bamboo coins.

It could be
full of nonsense,
old bikes
and Jehovah's witnesses…

When I pull back the door
the moonlight crinkles
the concrete floor

and a single toad
eats a fly

and the perfume of home
gathers me in its arms.

This is where
I learnt the alphabet

and ran like a
choo-choo train

into my
adult-
hood.

Red

The traffic light he had rigged
to the book shelf
is stuck—
a permanent, angry red.

Left behind—
two books on chess theory
and a robotics manual.

Over the chair
a torn, leather jacket.

And a carton of empty
cigarette packets.

'He has never had a girlfriend,'
his mother said.

'Been in this rooming house
for fifteen years.'

A life was over
or had he run away?

'Stop, look deeper,'
the traffic light said…

but nothing was messed up—
only a half-eaten piece of cake
on the desk.

The police knocked on
all the other doors
but no one would answer.

However, in the letterboxes
twenty dollar notes
had been placed in each…

If you listen closely
the echo of his footsteps
lingers on the stairs.

'He had never been close to anyone growing up
though he was fond of footy cards.'

The woman folded herself into
a porch chair

and pulled her cardigan close;
fending off the idea
she knew nothing about
his present life.

Autism
and no real conversation.

How it stopped everything.

'We'll have to take the traffic light,'
the officer said

'and if he turns up again
he'll be charged with theft.'

The woman nodded.
It made no difference.

Her mind was filled
by his favourite colour
and a longing…

Journey out the back door…

Have you ever seen slugs converse
about eternity?

How they squish out their messages
in silvery stains o-
ver concrete

their letters like spiderweb
tinsel—lean this way and
that. Their calculations

like a maze. Does it exist
or not? Probabilities and
strange mathematical
equations that change

depending on the medium
they traverse…

Or the angle of the sun.

Once, my sister spent
eons studying the path
of snails (the shells
made all the difference

to her) and stuck them
on aluminium sheeting
to see which direction
they would take…

while outside
my father's
heavy boot
crushed shells…

But to me,
snails
with their portable homes
never discuss
if eternity
exists

in their wide shell wonderings…

Oh but slugs,
those homeless, vagabonds

whisper and confetti
the place
with so many
questions…

Sometimes, I would like
to be a slug

and spray paint my thoughts
in archaic, undecipherable
symbols

without the label
of crazy…

Arthritis, Boats and Red Jam

My head feels like it's got arthritis —
swells up like a donut

and from the hole,
all my memories escape…

They go like ships
into the distance —

rowing, rowdy and gang-ho.
They shout about my

dictator ways.
How I never let them

out to play.
Would you?

The memory of
being stood up

beats its chest
and screams

'row on boys
row on'.

The kitten memory
of standing with an

empty container
at show and tell

vomits over the
side,

like a
convict

not used to
the sea…

My memory
of rape

just pollutes
around the edges

like a noxious
gas

ready to kill
anyone who comes near…

I get into a dinghy
and row in the opposite direction.

Head—a boiling donut,
magma memories

bubbling out
like red jam…

What poetry does

Poetry goes with small steps
to put a bomb in language.

It takes off with sails
and flies like a jet engine

around a tree—tethered to a point.
Its teeth bite and sting.

It hits you like
a wall,

whacks a punch
and haunts you.

It twists like washing in the wind
and eats snails like a garbage bin.

It carries a handbag of toothpicks
and mint gum

to undo you dear reader
and stick you together again

like a voodoo doll without
the death-threat.

Bite

Deep in the straggly reeds
away from the dawning sun
the young, scarred poet
has placed a tremulous little fish
that's there to conceal
a metaphorical handle

into the future—a handle
that meanders back through the reeds.
It's there to conceal
from the hot, yellow sun
the tremulous little fish
that the poet

the poor, innocent poet
placed without a handle
on understanding how the fish
could slip through the reeds
and out into the sun—
where there are no shadows to conceal

its little life in the balance. Nothing conceals
it but the pen of the poet
goes on with the light of the sun
opening the handle
of death wondering through the reeds.
Poor little fish.

Oh poor, little fish.
The hook in its mouth conceals
nothing from the dying reeds
and the poet
sags under the enormous handle
of the burning sun,

that horrible, burning sun
enlarged even further in fish
eyes that cannot handle
all that above water should be concealed.
And the poet
goes back to watching the reeds

that pour in the sun. 'Those reeds
where fish should always be,' says the poet
but the handle of the rod is always concealed.

Dear Separation,

You come with bee eyes and sting me awake. The dishes lounge over the bench like kamikaze beacons. On the radio 'You don't own me' spills in from the window. 'That's right, Mister' I want to scream, marching my independent womanhood across the room. Outside, a blue wren flies off. 'Not you too,' I sigh.

It must be ice-cream time. I march out the door — hurricane carefully hidden behind makeup.

'Hello, Miss,' the postie says. 'Nice day.' In my head I snap 'What's so good about it?', like a kettle boiling over.

After smiling, (he could be my next Mister), I promptly remember you at the restaurant fiddling with your ring, looking like a slimy tycoon.

A branch snaps in the wind. I grab the post and am blown back inside,

feel like flotsam as I orbit my lounge room dropping tears like a snail's silvery remains.

On the letter — 'Dear Writer'. I drop the pile of them on the table and pen one of my own.

Dear Separation,
you haul me like a rocket
through brambles of emotion
as easily as if I were
a tarot card.

I imagine putting a soldier's suit on —
gun by my side.

*How I will hunt you down
you broken cabinet
with no purpose!*

I shake myself.
A train rumbles past
like the uncertainty principle
and I head back to bed —
shattered as a bombed city…

Like a Small City

The Meaning

They have tied my poem
to a chair.
They will not let it breathe
or go to the bathroom.

To escape,
my poem imagines
it is outside
collecting sticks

to burn their faces.
Then
it jumps the concrete
cracks

like they are trolls
trying to trap it
and speeds round
the corner

like a criminal
escaping sentences…
But no matter
how far it twists,

the students peer —
buildings of overwhelming
faces
plucking its

cogs apart
to find out
what it means
right now on Wednesday

at 4pm.

Dollies, War and Pillars

The Leftovers

When the men go off to war,
the neat rows of manicured lawns
grow wild...

Boys ride their bikes like
all fences are broken

and little girls pull their dollies a-
part
thinking of a father who may
never come back...

Eventually, the women roll up
the whole shemozzle

as easily as carpet,

move into trailer parks
where the rent is cheaper

and turn into sand pillars
cos they looked back (for a moment)
on happier times.

And the desert
eats the children
in a cloud
of dust...

The Backovers

They come with big guns strapped on.

Memories of
legs, arms
and the occasional head
crashing through air

hide in their psyche.

Half of them want to go back
to the adrenaline
and commands
that made life simpler.

While the other half
want the peace
of a coffin.

They come unprepared for families
and are islands of
automated fists and
vicious words.

The sand pillars
trickle sand from their
'she'll be right
uptight skin',

roll out the neighbourhood,
smile their crusty grins

but only the pop, pop, pop
of empty shells
greet them…

The Togetherers

The sun rises like a
sheep skin across the sky.

Everywhere there is light—
except on the veranda
of one little house

where beer bottles
smash
against the wall,

smallering the new children
into shaking
paint pots

under the table.

The sand pillar
of this house
topples

like a
cascading
ant hill

over and over again

as the soldier
sees only
enemy faces—

shoots the cat
and goes
inside…

Door banging
like the claws
of a monster.

At Four, Learning Poetry

My language wagon
trundles along—
spilling scrabble tiles
plop, plop, plop.

I lurch forward
bouncing over weeds—
stop/start
across the footpath.

Overhead,
the clouds are
neatly ploughed
rows.

One lone seagull
picks at the letters
I leave behind—
yes/no

until words form:
'as' and 'no'
like islands
of sense.

It puts its head
to the side,
picks at my shadow
and caws at the wind.

Then suddenly,
a whole pack
of them
raid my wagon

and I am left
empty
as a letter
without a sentence.

Then just as suddenly,
they all flock off—
lumpy porridge
leaving only

'w all fa l'…

How to Write a Poem in a Time of Argument

You can't start just anywhere.
Do you begin with…

the curtains billowing innocently
in the wind. Toys stream like

gobbly-goo across the floor. One roller skate
stands nonchalantly in the doorway…

or do you start with a collapsed tree
taking off the corner of the house

unexpectedly in the middle of the
night like a thief shattering a window

so other things escape leaving soot
and debris piled up in the marriage.

Or do you begin with the night before
when romance blossomed like a cactus

flower—rare and beautiful in a house
full of children. No start at the beginning

when voices whined like helicopter rotors
around the same old, tired argument.

… and there's a banging of cupboard doors.
The baby crying in his high-chair.

The twins running around like
flying missiles—swords pointing

at each other moments from
catastrophe and then he starts

griping about your parenting skills
in a house of ADHD and special needs.

You are not well and are as fatigued
as if a dinosaur sits on your chest

and you haul the dishcloth at him
'Here you wash up then.'

He dodges and goes on banging cupboards
'I'm trying to make lunch.'

The phone goes and you fall over
the chair leg dodging a child

and then just like that
he is helping you up

and the argument is over
as one of the boys climbs through

the shattered window
and it's all hands on deck

to catch him and the poem
pulls up a chair and sits down to wait…

The girl-moth

The girl-moth looks up, sees a white hole
in the darkness above her
where
anything could fall in,
anything could be blown out—
and her plain, brown wings spasm.
Again she feels the pain of that cut.

She huddles down onto her pin-size shadow
where she keeps half a conversation,
two train tickets from her first and only date with man-moth
and a little sliver of her own wing.

Up above
anything could fall in,
anything could be blown out.

If it were last night
she'd fly up and out to investigate.
But now she is heavy, heavy
with something new and unexpected.

Last night's train hurtles backwards
'I love you,' he had said
but it was as untrustworthy
as the third rail.

The white hole menaces larger.
She looks again at her own piece of wing
and remembers how he said he had no time to wait
for tomorrow.

The New Beginning

All through the night
for many, many years
the terror, the terror.
Everywhere
round the room. How it

leered me from nightmares. And
I
veiled
in sweat and a
nattering of teeth, found the
ghost of my past

welding his fists.
Insecure, I couldn't turn out the light.
The past was always here —
hiding inside myself. That man was

always here again and again.

Prince 'I'm in charge'
screaming threats.
'You can't escape me' and
constantly using his fists.
Habitually stopping my progress,
obstructing my soul.
Prince 'I'm in charge'
and round and round. You became
the death of my
heart and self-belief.

Like a Small City

You had everything your way —
over the top perfect while I was
utterly demoted to second class.

But,
evening
comes in its dust of pink
over all
mountains like you.
Everyone

sees it the same.
Over all
mountains.
Evoluting
the
heart
into
new
growth. Little flower,

something has begun.
The
ring
of
new
growth and the finality of escape.
Every person who knows the fist of a psychopath is
reborn and regrown into new strength.

Four Vignettes

'Dear Noose,'

        he writes with a craggy, rheumatic hand
        while looking across the lake.
        The sun folds into the water like a swan
        div-
        ing
        for
        dark

        and the submarine of his heart
        slips
        closer
        into launch-
        ing.

        How would it be—
        blackness like a vice on his neck,
        blackness like the inside of a cockroach,
        blackness like the weight of tar
        pouring into his mouth.

        If only he could stop those voices
        laughing like demonic clowns.

        The trees bend like slingshots
        at Heaven where he wants to go

        and he imagines
        cannon-
        balling
        through the air.
        A rippling wave of blackness
        without a net.

One last hurrah
for everyone to laugh at.

Then the blackness of the hearse
travels through his mind.
All the faces of his children
lining
the side
of the
road—

giant stop signs
stepping all over
the mangled remains
of his life.

Now his rheumatic fingers
can barely hold
the numbered conversation
he so desperately wants.

Fly Traps and Spiders

She feels like a Venus Fly Trap
always choking
whenever she eats.

The scales clock no change
but still she purges.

All the boys'
wondering hands
haunt like
spiders.

She'd like to trap them
in her Venus Fly Trap
she had four years ago.

Now she can't look after anything.
Even the daisies die
as she ritually tries to eat
only one calorie a day.

She looks in the mirror—
yellow and thin—
a daisy.

But it's never enough.

The Eat Everything Life

                        Before, he sat
                        in his blow-up
                        arm chair

                laughing at the wind

                            then

                    an alien moth
                        attacked—

        big as a hippopotamus
                It shadowed him
                        like a
                          plane

and put all his fire out.

He huddles down into

> his amino acids
> chanting
> 'not real, not real'
>
> but the wing clips him
> and he falls unconscious
>
> with groans the size of
> houses.
>
> When he wakes—
> flowers walk past
> like everything is
> normal.

The Locked Ward

I sit here waiting for a bed
still as a corpse.
(if I do not move
the crows may not peck me
a-
part).

Elsewhere
a drug affected man
punches
a man
o-
ver
a chair

and the crying pool of women
greekly go
to rooms
eons

a-
way.

The cigarette smokers
plant their faces on
the window
like smudges of pain

as doors lock like
heavy kicks to the
air.

I expect prison wardens
to come round the corner
jangling keys
of sarcastic comments

or Frankenstein demons
to slice my head o-
pen
for assassination.

The trees scream in the distance
while a trolley rattles down
the hallway

talking like a ghost
about blood tests,
euthanasia
and
old shoes.

I had packed a bag
for Antarctica
where the voices said
'people would not be hurt

by all the demons coming in
to eat my soul'.

I would go peacefully
into the ice
where it would be too cold
and too white for hallucinations
to survive…

and there I would
bury my-
self

and melt into
white—
hugging close
to my belief
in God
like a stalagmite
to a stalactite…

In a crevasse
of space

I would
watch
new moss
bloom again.

Instead, my navy bag
sits next to me
like a
beached whale
out of sanity

while the door locks
every passer through

like a time card
punching
in
the arrival of
new
monsters…

On Becoming a Poet

First, I sloshed around,
muddy snowwoman—

my mind,
a puzzle
missing pieces.

The sun would
striate my pages,
eat my ink
and burn my heart.

Then I'd read something fantastic
and pop my head
back
in the oven of mediocrity.

Where were the words?

All over the place
like frilled neck lizards

they fought like
tattered wallpaper

in a mind
only half lit up.

Then the years passed
like mixing cakes

and my head started
stringing sentences out

till they sang like
piano keys
almost in tune.

Now I have these
little creations—

ordered and fat
roasted
with language…

The Horse that Knows More

Words fall into my mouth like
rocks
and I get stuck like glue.
I point to the car
buzzing along outside

and say
'kettle hat with wheels'.

The wattle shakes its head like
a horse that knows more.

I fall back in time
when the grand kids used to come…

Monopoly would be on the floor

and I'd sit rocking thoughtfully
over my turn
and the deals I'd like to make.

My husband puts his arm
around me
and I am contentment,
stop trying to talk
and squeeze his hand.

The curtains billow
in the breeze like
two cotton
hugs.

My husband sighs
and goes to make tea.

Words fall into my mouth like
rocks.
I want to tell him…

but all that comes out is:
'chickens will grow greener'
and
'grass will get wings'.

The Last Day

> *'The wick of youth being burned and the oil spent—'*
> *The Living Beauty, W.B Yeats*

She bends over her desk, a carcass in the making,
licking stamps for retirement home brochures.

On the floor, ants pile up like strands of liquorice
as she sits in her wheelchair, back bent like Houdini

out of her shirt and into the cold. The milky way
she got at sixteen is now a faded, crinkly galaxy

that holds the memory of when a god touched her
seventy-two years ago when locomotives were in.

She remembers the child she pushed on the swing
but not the name of the fully-grown woman

who came yesterday she thinks but not the
day before and then there's the mysterious man

who creeps around the edge of her life and claims to be
David. But he just looks too big and grown to be

her son and she thinks he's after something else
and often bats him away with her yellow purse

or her woollen hat but misses every time
as he sits too far away. But secretly she likes the

attention and waits like a hang-glider in mid-air
for a-noth-er vis-it—

hands like doilies between things
like not getting tea and forgetting

what she is after and ending up
with cactus flowers instead.

Outside, the sun buries itself behind
the trees and the houses

like a carriage going the wrong way.
While the nurse wheels her to the dining room,

the old lady says how she's looking
for the perfect home and drops envelopes

like a card filing system back
to her room and the nurse is talking

of Hansel and Gretel but she's not
listening. Instead she watches the carriage

going the wrong way. Screams in her heart.
And that evening the candle is spent…

Womb

'I don't want it,' he said—
anger like a V8 jack-knifing down the highway.
Anger like a rocket bursting into flame.
Anger like a tsunami flattening buildings.
Anger. He was just so big with it.

The girl shivered inside
like she was a fly
with her wings
sardonically pulled off.

And in the evening light,
her shadow
fell
off the wall
and slid
onto the floor.

Over on the balcony,
two empty lounge chairs
watched
the sun
turn a sand bank
red
like a bloody womb.

Then the waves
crashed
sand
from the edges
of it
and the girl felt
sick.

It was always like this.

On Encouragement

You always come after the writing
in your pink bonnet and chardonnay glasses

but what about before
when I am stuck in a cave—
dead fish paper on the walls,

ink sprawling out like maggots
of half-formed words…

The time when I am trapped
in the quicksand of uncertainty.

Where are you then
oh gentle, brass band?

If only I could bottle you
and live on your essence,
I'd be a lighthouse
in my miserable cave

and words would rise
like ghosts
and parade under-
neath
my door

like smoky steps
of luck, hope and possibility.

About the Author

Carla de Goede has one book of poetry, *Those Hairy Letters* published by Melbourne Poets' Union. In manuscript form, *Like a Small City* was short-listed for the 2022 Dorothy Hewett Award.

Her work has been published in various literary magazines including *Blue Dog* and *Said the Rat,* and she has been a featured reader and won or been short-listed in various poetry competitions.

Like a Small City is the first collection published by **in case of emergency press**.